HAL•LEONARD® DRUM PLAY-ALONG™

AUDIO ACCESS INCLUDED

MORE SONGS FOR BEGINNERS

Play 8 Songs with Sound-alike Audio

Page	Title
2	Boulevard of Broken Dreams GREEN DAY
6	Free Fallin' TOM PETTY
14	Man in the Box ALICE IN CHAINS
18	Simple Man LYNYRD SKYNYRD
9	Sunshine of Your Love CREAM
24	Sweet Child O' Mine GUNS N' ROSES
31	Ticket to Ride THE BEATLES
34	You Shook Me All Night Long AC/DC

PLAYBACK+
Speed • Pitch • Balance • Loop

To access audio visit:
www.halleonard.com/mylibrary

3745-1738-4287-8271

ISBN 978-1-5400-2976-8

Visit Hal Leonard Online at
www.halleonard.com

Contact Us:
Hal Leonard
7777 West Bluemound Road
Milwaukee, WI 53213
Email: info@halleonard.com

In Europe contact:
Hal Leonard Europe Limited
42 Wigmore Street
Marylebone, London, W1U 2RN
Email: info@halleonardeurope.com

In Australia contact:
Hal Leonard Australia Pty. Ltd.
4 Lentara Court
Cheltenham, Victoria, 3192 Australia
Email: info@halleonard.com.au

Boulevard of Broken Dreams

Words by Billie Joe
Music by Green Day

Intro
Moderately slow ♩ = 84

𝄋 Verse

2nd time, substitute Fill 1

1. I walk a lone - ly road,   the on - ly one that I ___ have ev - er known. ___
2. *See additional lyrics*

___ Don't know where it goes,   but it's home to me ___ and I walk a - lone. ___

I walk this emp - ty street   on the bou - le - vard ___ of bro - ken dreams, ___

Fill 1

when the cit - y sleeps and I'm the on - ly one _ and I walk a - lone. __

I walk a - lone, _ I walk a - lone. ___

I walk a - lone, _ I walk a...

Chorus

2nd time, substitute Fill 2

My shad - ow's on - ly one that walks _ be - side me.

My shal - low heart's _

_ the on - ly thing _ that's beat - ing.

Some - times _ I wish _ some - one up there _ will find me.

To Coda

Till then ___ I walk ___ a - lone.

Interlude

Ah, ___ ah, ___ ah, ___ ah. _____ Ah, ___ ah, ___

Fill 2

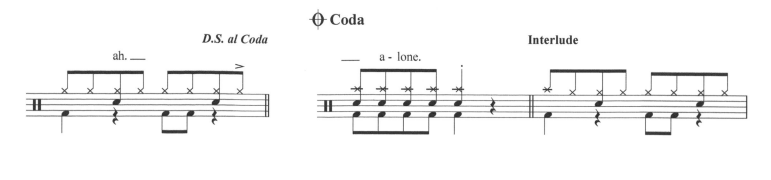

⊕ Coda

D.S. al Coda

ah. ____

Interlude

____ a - lone.

I walk a-lone, ___ I walk a...

Guitar Solo

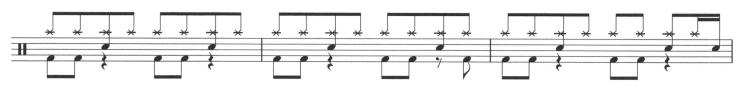

Verse

3. I walk this emp - ty street on the bou - le - vard ___ of bro - ken dreams, ___

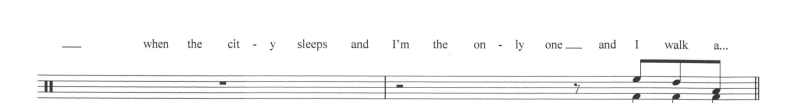

____ when the cit - y sleeps and I'm the on - ly one ___ and I walk a...

Chorus

Outro

Additional Lyrics

2. I'm walkin' down the line that divides me somewhere in my mind.
   On the borderline of the edge and where I walk alone.
   Read between the lines, what's fucked up and ev'rything's alright.
   Check my vital signs to know I'm still alive and I walk alone.
   I walk alone, I walk alone.
   I walk alone, I walk a...

Free Fallin'

Words and Music by Tom Petty and Jeff Lynne

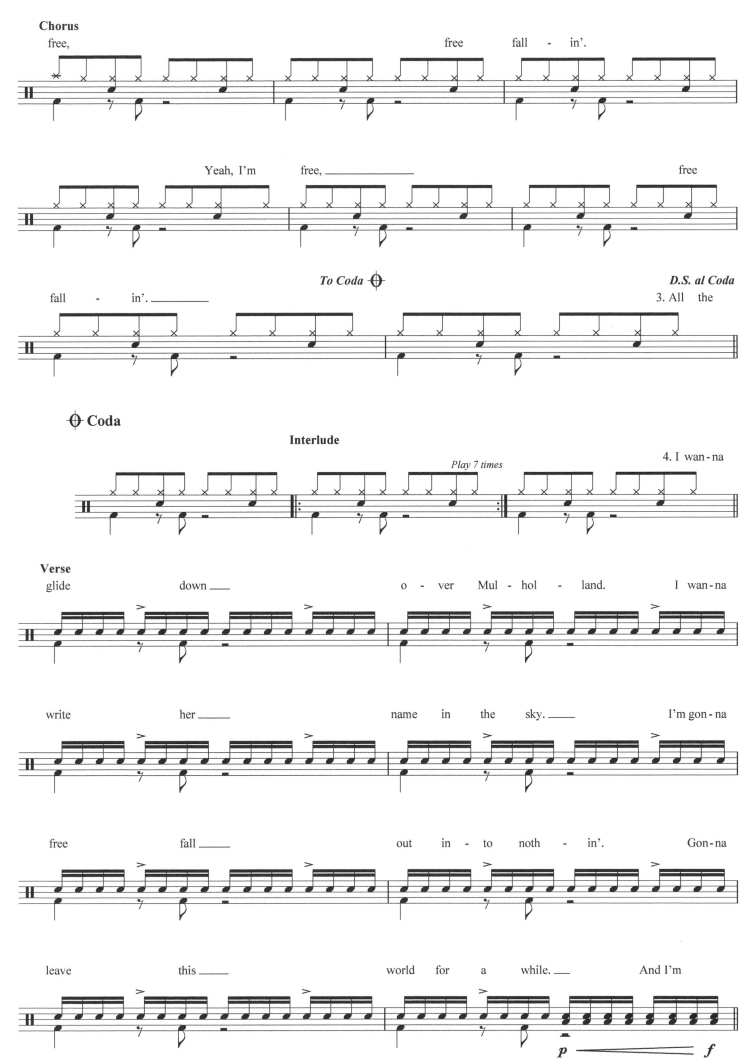

Chorus

Additional Lyrics

3. All the vampires walkin' through the valley
   Move west down Ventura Boulevard.
   And all the bad boys are standin' in the shadows.
   And the good girls are home with broken hearts.

Sunshine of Your Love

Words and Music by Eric Clapton, Jack Bruce and Pete Brown

Intro
Moderately ♩ = 112

1. It's

Play 3 times

Verse

get - ting near dawn, _ when lights close their ti - red eyes. _

_ I'll soon be with you, _ my _ love, _

give you my dawn _ sur - prise. _____ I'll be with you, dar - ling, soon. _

_ I'll be with you when _ the stars _ start _ fall - ing.

I'll stay with you till ___ my ___ seas ___ are ___ dried ___ up. ___

Chorus

I've ___ been wait - ing so ___ long

to ___ be where ___ I'm go - in', in ___ the sun -

- shine of ___ your love. ___

Guitar Solo

Play 7 times

Play 3 times

Verse

3. I'm   with   you,   my   love, _____   the

light's shin-ing through __ on __ you. _____   Yes, I'm   with you, my   love. ____

It's the   morn-ing and just __ we   two. _____   I'll

stay with you, dar - ling, now. ___ I'll stay with you till ___ my seas ___

___ are ___ dried ___ up. _____

Play 3 times

Chorus

I've ___ been wait - ing so ___ long, I've ___ been wait -

- ing ___ so long, ___ I've ___ been wait - ing so ___ long

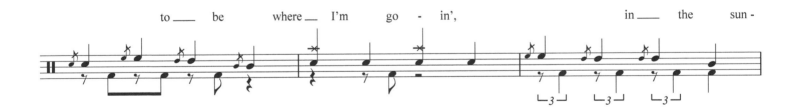

to ___ be where ___ I'm go - in', in ___ the sun -

- shine of ___ your love. _____

Repeat and fade

Man in the Box

Written by Jerry Cantrell and Layne Staley

Intro
Moderately ♩ = 105

Ah,   ah,   ah,

ah,   ah,   ah,   ah,   ah,   ah.

Ah,   ah,   ah,   ah,   ah,   ah,   ah,   ah,   ah.

Verse
I'm   the man   in the box,
2. *See additional lyrics*

bur - ied in

my shit.

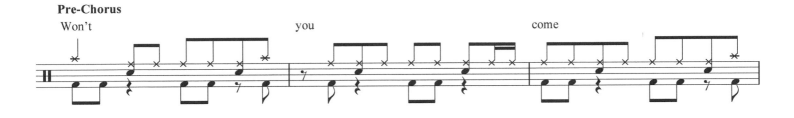

Pre-Chorus

Won't you come

and _____ save ___ me? Save _

𝄋 **Chorus**

2nd time, substitute Fill 1

___ me. _____ Feed _____

_____ my eyes, ___ can ___ you sew ___ them shut?

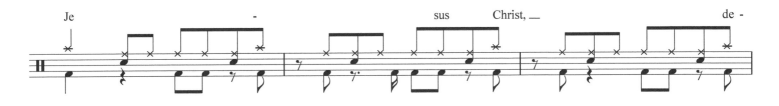

Je - sus Christ, ___ de -

Fill 1

D.S. al Coda   Coda

you've sewn ___ them ___ shut.

Outro

Ah,   ah, ___   ah,   ah,   ah, ___   ah,   ah,   ah, ___   ah.

___

Ah,   ah, ___   ah,   ah,   ah, ___   ah,

ah,   ah, ___   ah. _____

Additional Lyrics

2. I'm the dog who gets beat.
Shove my nose in shit.

Simple Man

Words and Music by Ronnie Van Zant and Gary Rossington

Intro
Slowly ♩ = 60

1. My ma - ma

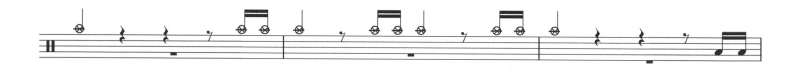

Verse

told me,   when I was — young, —   "Come sit be -

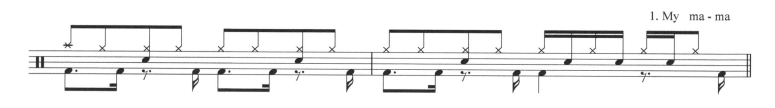

side me,   my on - ly — son, —   and lis - ten

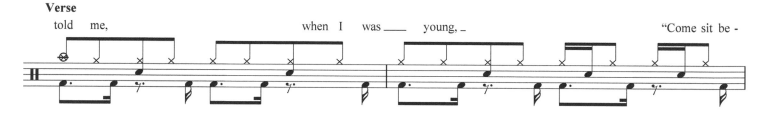

close - ly   to what I — say. —   And if you

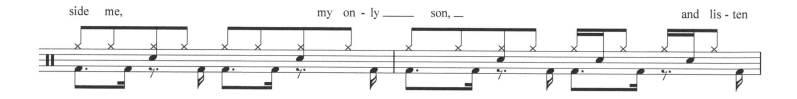

do this,   it - 'll help you   some ____ sun - ny day. ____

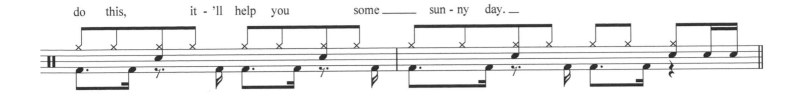

Interlude

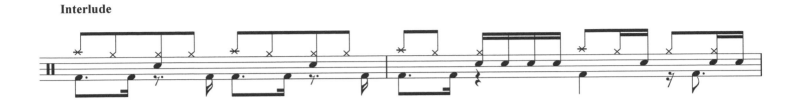

2. Oh, take your

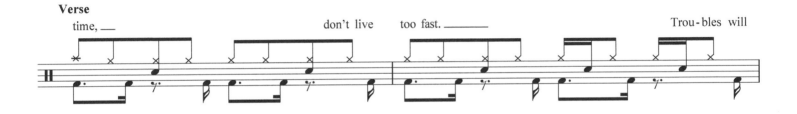

Verse

time, ____   don't live   too fast. _____   Trou - bles will

come, ____   and they will ____ pass. _____   Go find a

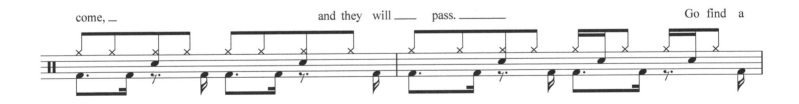

wom - an,   and you'll find ____ love. _____   And don't for -

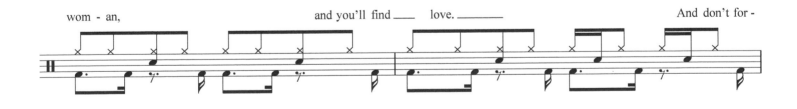

get, son,   there is ____ some - one   up _____ a - bove.   And be a

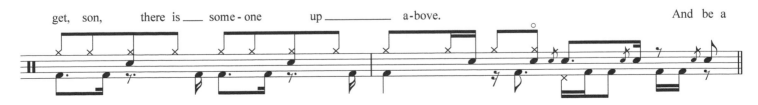

do this, oh, ba - by, if you try. _____ All that I

want for_ you, my son, _ is to be _____ sat - is - fied. _____ And be a

𝄋 Chorus
sim - ple _____ kind of _____ man. _____ Oh, be

some - thin' ___ you love and un - der - stand. _____ Ba - by, be a

sim - ple _____ kind of _____ man. Oh, won't you

To Coda 🟢
do this for me, son, if you can?" _____ Oh, yes, I will.

Guitar Solo

Verse

4. "Oh, don't you   wor - ry,   you'll find your-

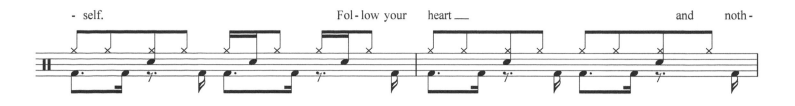

- self.   Fol - low your heart ____   and noth -

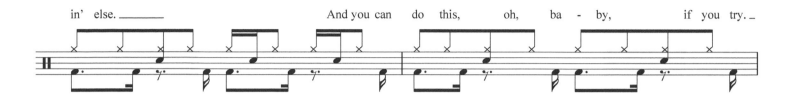

in' else. _____   And you can do this,   oh, ba - by,   if you try. __

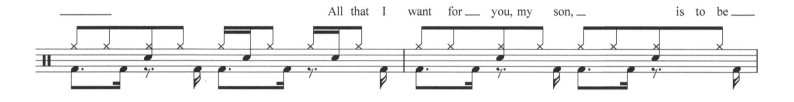

_____   All that I want for ___ you, my son, __   is to be ___

D.S. al Coda   ⊕ **Coda**

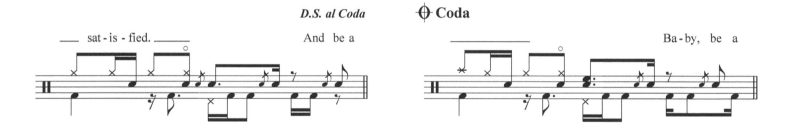

____ sat - is - fied. _____   And be a   _____   Ba - by, be a

Outro

Begin fade

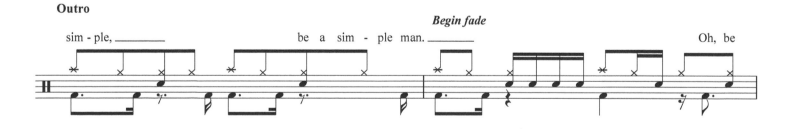

sim - ple, _____   be a sim - ple man. _____   Oh, be

Fade out

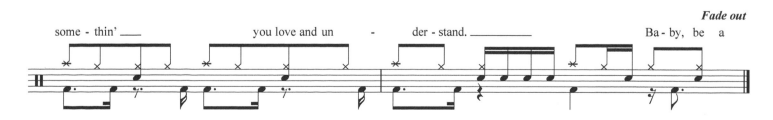

some - thin' ____   you love and un -   der - stand. _____   Ba - by, be a

Sweet Child O' Mine

Words and Music by W. Axl Rose, Slash,
Izzy Stradlin', Duff McKagan and Steven Adler

Intro
Moderate Rock ♩ = 122

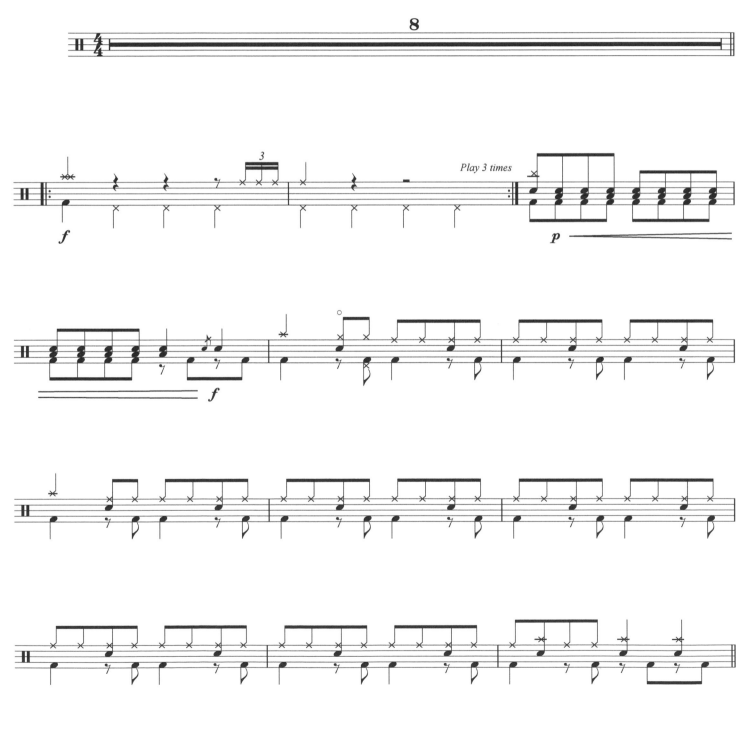

Verse

1. She's got a smile _ that it seems to me, _ re - minds _ me of child - hood

2. *See additional lyrics*

2nd time, substitute Fill 1

mem - o - ries _ where ev - 'ry - thing _ was as fresh _ as the bright, _ blue sky. _

_____ Now and then, _ when I

see her face, _ she takes me a - way _ to that

2nd time, substitute Fill 2

spe - cial place. _ And if I

2nd time, substitute Fill 2

stare _ too _ long, I'd prob - 'bly break down and cry. _____

Chorus

Whoa, whoa, _ whoa, _ sweet child of mine. _

_____ Whoa, oh, oh, oh, __

Fill 1

Fill 2

sweet love of mine. __

Guitar Solo

1.

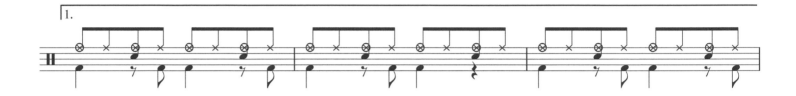

2.

Ooh, _____

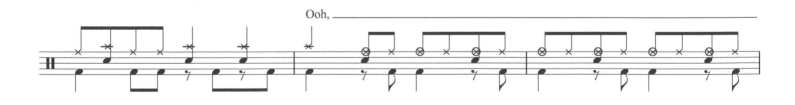

ah, _____

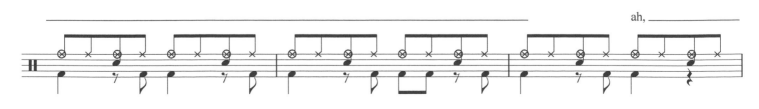

26

ooh, ah, ah, ah, yeah. _____

Chorus

Whoa, oh, oh, oh, _____ sweet child of mine. _____

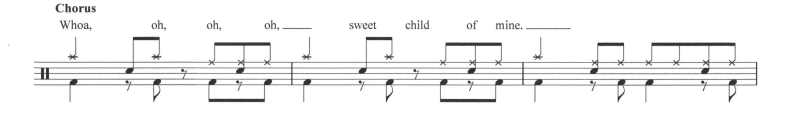

Ooh, whoa, oh, _____ oh, _____ sweet love of mine. _

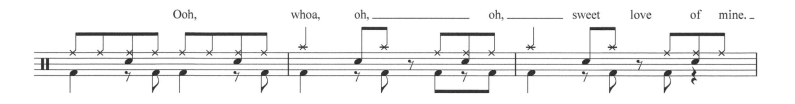

___ Whoa, oh, oh, oh, _

_____ sweet _ child _ of mine. _____ Ooh, _____ yeah. _____

Ooh, _____ sweet love of mine. _____

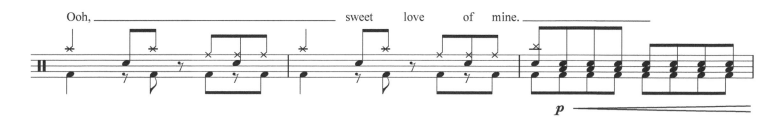

p

Guitar Solo

f

Play 4 times

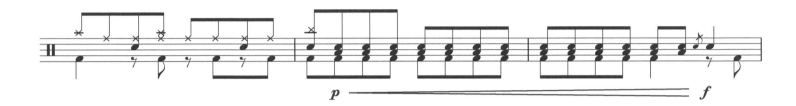

p ———————————————— *f*

Outro

Where do we go? __   Where do we go __ now?

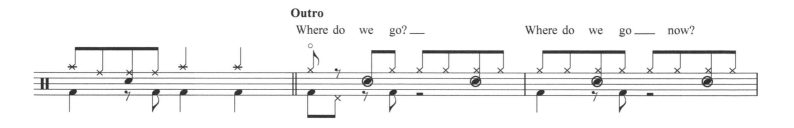

Where do we go? __   Mm, mm, oh, __ where do we go? __

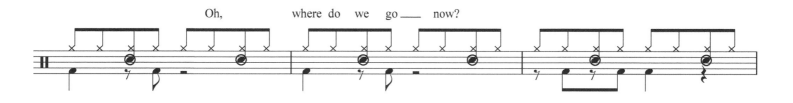

Oh,   where do we go __ now?

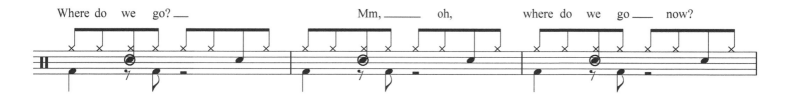

Where do we go? __   Mm, __ oh,   where do we go __ now?

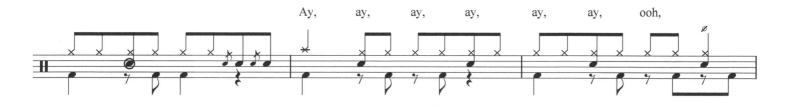

Ay, ay, ay, ay, ay, ay, ooh,

where do we go __ now? Ah, ah, ah, ah, ah, oh, __ oh. __ Where do we go? __

p —————————— *f*

Additional lyrics

2. She's got eyes of the bluest skies
As if they thought of rain.
I'd hate to look into those eyes
And see an ounce of pain.
Her hair reminds me of a warm, safe place
Where as a child I'd hide,
And pray for the thunder and the rain
To quietly pass me by.

Ticket to Ride

Words and Music by John Lennon and Paul McCartney

Additional Lyrics

2., 4. She said that living with me
Is bringing her down, yeah!
She would never be free
When I was around.

You Shook Me All Night Long

Words and Music by Angus Young, Malcolm Young and Brian Johnson

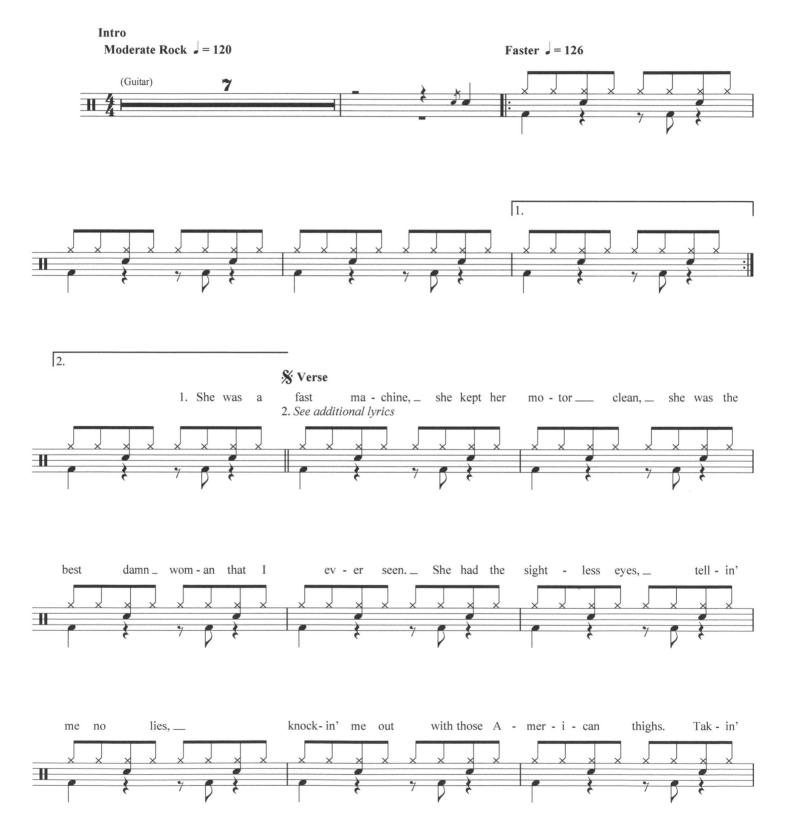

Intro
Moderate Rock ♩ = 120

(Guitar)

Faster ♩ = 126

1.

2.

𝄋 Verse

1. She was a   fast   ma - chine, __   she kept her   mo - tor __   clean, __   she was the
2. *See additional lyrics*

best   damn __   wom - an   that I   ev - er   seen. __   She had the   sight - less   eyes, __   tell - in'

me   no   lies, __   knock - in'   me   out   with those   A - mer - i - can   thighs.   Tak - in'

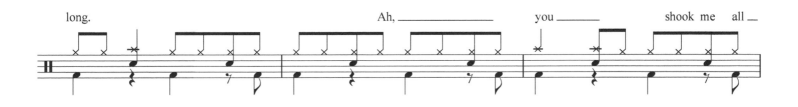

Outro-Chorus

You real - ly took me, and you   shook me all _____   night _

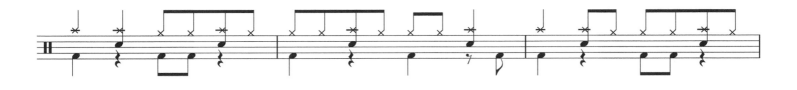

long.   Ah, _____   you _____   shook me all _

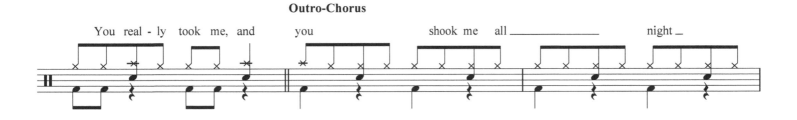

_____   night _   long.   Yeah, _ yeah, _ you _

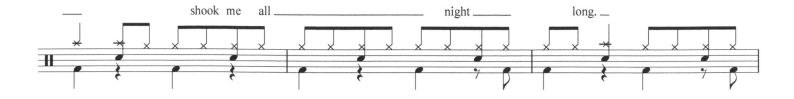

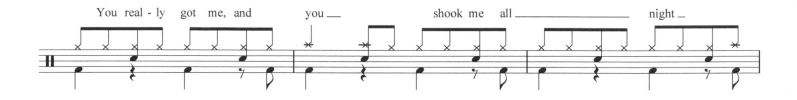

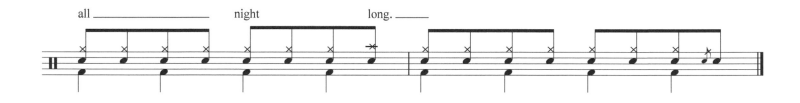

Additional Lyrics

2. Workin' double-time on the seduction line.
She was one of a kind; she's just a mine, all mine.
Wanted no applause; just another cause.
Made a meal out of me, and come back for more.
Had to cool me down to take another round.
Now I'm back in the ring to take another swing.
'Cause the walls was shakin', the earth was quakin',
My mind was achin', and we were makin' it. And you...

HAL•LEONARD® DRUM PLAY-ALONG

The Drum Play-Along™ Series will help you play your favorite songs quickly and easily! Just follow the drum notation, listen to the audio to hear how the drums should sound, and then play-along using the separate backing tracks. The lyrics are also included for reference. The audio files are enhanced so you can adjust the recording to any tempo without changing pitch!

1. Pop/Rock
00699742.....................$14.99

2. Classic Rock
00699741.....................$16.99

3. Hard Rock
00699743.....................$17.99

4. Modern Rock
00699744.....................$19.99

5. Funk
00699745.....................$16.99

7. Punk Rock
00699747.....................$14.99

8. '80s Rock
00699832.....................$16.99

9. Cover Band Hits
00211599.....................$16.99

10. blink-182
00699834.....................$19.99

11. Jimi Hendrix Experience: Smash Hits
00699835.....................$19.99

12. The Police
00700268.....................$16.99

13. Steely Dan
00700202.....................$17.99

15. The Beatles
00256656.....................$17.99

16. Blues
00700272.....................$17.99

17. Nirvana
00700273.....................$16.99

18. Motown
00700274.....................$16.99

19. Rock Band: Modern Rock Edition
00700707.....................$17.99

21. Weezer
00700959.....................$14.99

22. Black Sabbath
00701190.....................$17.99

23. The Who
00701191.....................$22.99

24. Pink Floyd – Dark Side of the Moon
00701612.....................$19.99

25. Bob Marley
00701703.....................$19.99

26. Aerosmith
00701887.....................$19.99

27. Modern Worship
00701921.....................$19.99

29. Queen
00702389.....................$17.99

30. Dream Theater
00111942.....................$24.99

31. Red Hot Chili Peppers
00702992.....................$19.99

32. Songs for Beginners
00704204.....................$15.99

33. James Brown
00117422.....................$17.99

34. U2
00124470.....................$19.99

35. Buddy Rich
00124640.....................$19.99

36. Wipe Out & 7 Other Fun Songs
00125341.....................$19.99

37. Slayer
00139861.....................$17.99

38. Eagles
00143920.....................$17.99

39. Kiss
00143937.....................$16.99

40. Stevie Ray Vaughan
00146155.....................$16.99

41. Rock Songs for Kids
00148113.....................$15.99

42. Easy Rock Songs
00148143.....................$15.99

45. Bon Jovi
00200891.....................$17.99

46. Mötley Crüe
00200892.....................$16.99

47. Metallica: 1983-1988
00234340.....................$19.99

48. Metallica: 1991-2016
00234341.....................$19.99

49. Top Rock Hits
00256655.....................$16.99

51. Deep Purple
00278400.....................$16.99

52. More Songs for Beginners
00278403.....................$14.99

53. Pop Songs for Kids
00298650.....................$15.99

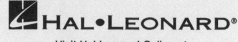

Visit Hal Leonard Online at
www.halleonard.com

Prices, contents and availability subject to change without notice and may vary outside the US.

DRUM TRANSCRIPTIONS
FROM HAL LEONARD

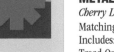

THE BEATLES DRUM COLLECTION
26 drum transcriptions of some of the Beatles' best, including: Back in the U.S.S.R. • Birthday • Can't Buy Me Love • Eight Days a Week • Help! • Helter Skelter • I Saw Her Standing There • Ob-La-Di, Ob-La-Da • Paperback Writer • Revolution • Sgt. Pepper's Lonely Hearts Club Band • Something • Twist and Shout • and more.
00690402 . . . . $19.99

BEST OF BLINK-182
Features Travis Barker's bashing beats from a baker's dozen of Blink's best. Songs: Adam's Song • Aliens Exist • All the Small Things • Anthem Part II • Dammit • Don't Leave Me • Dumpweed • First Date • Josie • Pathetic • The Rock Show • Stay Together for the Kids • What's My Age Again?
00690621 . . . . $22.99

DRUM CHART HITS
Authentic drum transcriptions of 30 pop and rock hits are including: Can't Stop the Feeling • Ex's & Oh's • Get Lucky • Moves like Jagger • Shake It Off • Thinking Out Loud • 24K Magic • Uptown Funk • and more.
00234062 . . . . $17.99

INCUBUS DRUM COLLECTION
Drum transcriptions for 13 of the biggest hits from this alt-metal band. Includes: Are You In? • Blood on the Ground • Circles • A Crow Left of the Murder • Drive • Megalomaniac • Nice to Know You • Pardon Me • Privilege • Stellar • Talk Shows on Mute • Wish You Were Here • Zee Deveel.
00690763 . . . . $17.95

BEST OF THE DAVE MATTHEWS BAND FOR DRUMS
Cherry Lane Music
Note-for-note transcriptions of Carter Beauford's great drum work: The Best of What's Around • Crash into Me • What Would You Say.
02500184 . . . . $19.95

DAVE MATTHEWS BAND – FAN FAVORITES FOR DRUMS
Cherry Lane Music
Exact drum transcriptions of every Carter Beauford beat from 10 of the most requested DMB hits: Crush • Dancing Nancies • Everyday • Grey Street • Jimi Thing • The Space Between • Tripping Billies • Two Step • Warehouse • Where Are You Going.
02500643 . . . . $19.95

METALLICA – …AND JUSTICE FOR ALL
Cherry Lane Music
Drum transcriptions to every song from Metallica's blockbuster album, plus complete drum setup diagrams, and background notes on Lars Ulrich's drumming style.
02503504 . . . . $19.99

METALLICA – BLACK
Cherry Lane Music
Matching folio to their critically acclaimed self-titled album. Includes: Enter Sandman * Sad But True * The Unforgiven * Don't Tread On Me * Of Wolf And Man * The God That Failed * Nothing Else Matters * and 5 more metal crunchers.
02503509 . . . . $22.99

METALLICA – MASTER OF PUPPETS
Cherry Lane Music
Matching folio to the best-selling album. Includes: Master Of Puppets • Battery • Leper Messiah • plus photos.
02503502 . . . . $19.99

METALLICA – RIDE THE LIGHTNING
Cherry Lane Music
Matching folio to Metallica's second album, including: Creeping Death • Fade To Black • and more.
02503507 . . . . $19.99

NIRVANA DRUM COLLECTION
Features transcriptions of Dave Grohl's actual drum tracks on 17 hits culled from four albums: *Bleach, Nevermind, Incesticide* and *In Utero*. Includes the songs: About a Girl • All Apologies • Blew • Come as You Are • Dumb • Heart Shaped Box • In Bloom • Lithium • (New Wave) Polly • Smells like Teen Spirit • and more. Also includes a drum notation legend.
00690316 . . . . $22.99

BEST OF RED HOT CHILI PEPPERS FOR DRUMS
Note-for-note drum transcriptions for every funky beat blasted by Chad Smith on 20 hits from *Mother's Milk* through *By the Way*! Includes: Aeroplane • Breaking the Girl • By the Way • Californication • Give It Away • Higher Ground • Knock Me Down • Me and My Friends • My Friends • Right on Time • Scar Tissue • Throw Away Your Television • True Men Don't Kill Coyotes • Under the Bridge • and more.
00690587 . . . . $24.99

RED HOT CHILI PEPPERS – GREATEST HITS
Essential for Peppers fans! Features Chad Smith's thunderous drumming transcribed note-for-note from their *Greatest Hits* album. 15 songs: Breaking the Girl • By the Way • Californication • Give It Away • Higher Ground • My Friends • Scar Tissue • Suck My Kiss • Under the Bridge • and more.
00690681 . . . . $22.99

RED HOT CHILI PEPPERS – I'M WITH YOU
Note-for-note drum transcriptions from the group's tenth album: The Adventures of Rain Dance Maggie • Annie Wants a Baby • Brendan's Death Song • Dance, Dance, Dance • Did I Let You Know • Ethiopia • Even You Brutus? • Factory of Faith • Goodbye Hooray • Happiness Loves Company • Look Around • Meet Me at the Corner • Monarchy of Roses • Police Station.
00691168 . . . . $22.99

RUSH – THE SPIRIT OF RADIO: GREATEST HITS 1974-1987
17 exact drum transcriptions from Neil Peart! Includes: Closer to the Heart • Fly by Night • Freewill • Limelight • Red Barchetta • Spirit of Radio • Subdivisions • Time Stand Still • Tom Sawyer • The Trees • Working Man • 2112 (I Overture & II Temples of Syrinx).
00323857 . . . . $22.99

HAL•LEONARD®
7777 W. BLUEMOUND RD. P.O. BOX 13819 MILWAUKEE, WI 53213

www.halleonard.com